Animals in the Wild

Whale and Dolphin

by Vincent Serventy

RSVP
**RAINTREE
STECK-VAUGHN**
P U B L I S H E R S
The Steck-Vaughn Company

Austin, Texas

Whales and dolphins have fins and live in the sea, but they are not fish. They are mammals. They must rise to the surface of the water to breathe air.

Whales, dolphins, and porpoises are
members of the same animal family.
Some of the family have teeth. Others do
not. They hunt their food underwater.

Blue whales can stay underwater for more
than half an hour. They may be as heavy as

twenty elephants. Blue whales can swim
almost twenty miles per hour.

Dolphins send out sounds to find food.
The sounds bounce back from whatever
they hit. Humans cannot hear them.

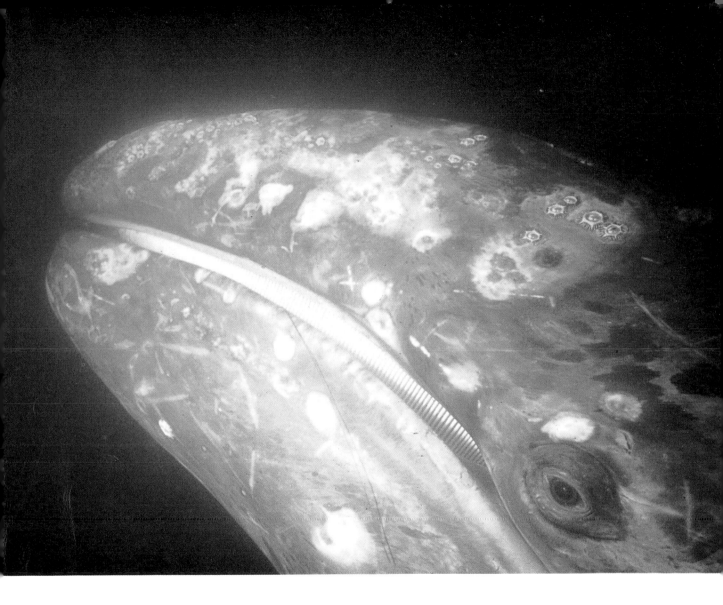

Toothless whales have horny plates called baleen. The plates have bristles that hold in shrimp and other food.

Humpback whales send out special songs
that can last twenty minutes. Humpback

whales can leap out of the water. The leaps
are called breaching.

Whales have tough, spongy skin. The fat under the skin is called blubber. It keeps whales warm in cold water.

Whale calves are born underwater, tail first.
Their mothers push them to the surface of
the water to breathe.

Most whales travel the same route through the seas every year. Whales and dolphins

like to stay with their own kind. Some even
travel in herds of up to one thousand.

Whales can be friendly toward humans.
Some allow people to pet them. Divers
swim safely near most whales and calves.

Dolphins are also friendly. There are many
stories about dolphins rescuing humans.
Dolphins are easily trained.

Whales sometimes strand themselves on beaches. They die out of the water.

Entire herds of whales have stranded
themselves. No one knows exactly why.

17

The largest of all toothed whales is the
sperm whale. Sperm whales can grow to

65 feet long and weigh almost 40 tons.
They can dive to almost 10,000 feet.

Orca whales live all over the world. They eat sharks, small whales, and sea lions. They tear their victims with their teeth.

Orcas are called killer whales because they
helped early Spanish whalers to hunt
other whales. They are very smart.

Dolphins have beaked heads and peg-like
teeth. Porpoises have rounder heads and

spade-like teeth. In some countries, it is
not legal to kill dolphins and whales.

First Steck-Vaughn Edition 1992

First published in the United States 1985
by Raintree Publishers, A Division of Steck-Vaughn Company.

Reprinted in 1989

First published in Australia in 1984 by
John Ferguson Pty. Ltd.
133 Macquarie Street
Sydney, NSW 2000

The North American hardcover edition published by arrangement
with Gareth Stevens Inc.

Acknowledgments are due to Vincent Serventy for all photographs in
this book except the following:
D. Hembre cover, p. 11; Earthviews, K.C. Balcomb p. 2; Marine Mammal
Fund, Robert Pitman p.3, 17; Earthviews, Richard Sears p. 4–5, 8–9,
12–13; Earthviews, Robert Pitman p. 6, 21, 22–3; Earthviews, Larry
Cochrane p. 7; Earthviews, Simone Morton Dangles p. 14; Ron and
Valerie Taylor p. 18–19.

Library of Congress number: 84-15118

Library of Congress Cataloging in Publication Data

Serventy, Vincent.
  Whale & dolphin.

  (Animals in the wild)
  Summary: Shows the whale and dolphin in their natural surroundings
and describes their life and struggle for survival.
    1. Whales—Juvenile literature. 2. Dolphins—Juvenile literature.
[1. Whales. 2. Dolphins]
I. Title. II. Title: Whale and dolphin. III. Series.
QL737.C4S46 1984   599.5   84-15118

ISBN 0-8172-2401-7   hardcover library binding

ISBN 0-8114-6892-5   softcover binding

  5 6 7 8 9 10 11 12 13   99 98 97 96 95 94 93